श्री शिव

শ্রী শিব পূজা

Śrī Śiva Pūjā

Beginner

The Worship of the Supreme Lord of Infinite Consciousness

by
Swami Satyananda Saraswati

शिव पूजा শিব পূজা Śiva Pūjā

by Devi Mandir Publications
5950 Highway 128
Napa, CA 94558 USA
Communications: Phone and Fax 1-707-966-2802
E-Mail swamiji@shreemaa.org
Please visit us on the World Wide Web at
http://www.shreemaa.org

ISBN 1-877795-27-5
Library of Congress Catalog Card Number
CIP 2001 126531

शिव पूजा শিব পূজা Śiva Pūjā
Swami Satyananda Saraswati
1. Hindu Religion. 2. Worship. 3. Spirituality.
4. Philosophy. I. Saraswati, Swami Satyananda;

शिव पूजा Śiva Pūjā শিব পূজা

Brahma, Vishnu and the Shiva Lingam

One day Brahma, the Creator, was walking down a path, when he met Lord Vishnu, the Protector, along the way. Not recognizing the Divine Lord, he enquired, "Who are you?"

"What do you mean, 'Who am I!'" responded Vishnu indignantly. "I am Vishnu, the Sustainer of All. Who are you who is asking?"

Brahma got angry and replied, "I am Brahma, the Creator of the Universe. You must show respect to me because I create everything that is."

And quite foolishly Brahma and Vishnu started to argue. Brahma said, "Unless I create, there will be nothing for you to preserve. You will have no work without me. You are totally dependent upon me."

Vishnu retorted, "You sprang from my navel, you ungrateful old man. If I cut your umbilical cord, you will be finished."

Right there where they were arguing, all of a sudden, up came a Shiva lingam, just there between them. And it kept growing and growing and growing until it went out of sight.

"What is this?" they were both surprised. "It appears to be a Shiva lingam."

"Alright," said Vishnu. "I'll tell you how we can settle this. Whoever can find the end of this Shiva lingam first, is the superior. Brahma, you go to the top, and I'll go to the bottom. The first one to reach the end will return to give the news. He will be the winner."

Vishnu became a boar and started down, following the Shiva lingam, burrowing down underneath the earth. He continued going down further and further and further.

"This lingam doesn't have an end," he thought. "It just keeps going and going. I'm tired, and I've had enough. I'm going back."

Brahma, on the other hand, got on his swan, and went up and up and up. He passed through the clouds and continued on towards the other end of infinity. As he was still going, he said in desperation, "When is this going to stop? Where is the end of this Shiva lingam?"

Just as he was getting near to what he thought must be the top, a flower fell down from Lord Shiva's head. As the flower fell, Brahma caught it, grabbed it in mid-air, and said, "Oh little flower, from where have you come?"

"I came from the head of Lord Shiva, replied the flower. "A devotee put me there as a token of worship, and a gust of wind came and knocked me off. I came from Shiva's head."

"Well," said Brahma, "I was just going up there to Shiva's head to get a flower, and it's so nice of you to come down here. Let me ask a little favor of you. Would you tell Vishnu that I took you off from the top of the Shiva lingam?"

"Well, that's not quite true," replied the little flower. "Actually, I fell off from the top of the Shiva lingam in a gust of wind."

Brahma said, "Do you know that I am Brahma, the Creator of the universe? If you just do this little thing for me, I will make sure that you are honored among all flowers."

He put the flower in his pocket, and went back down.

"Hello, Vishnu!" greeted Brahma. "Did you find the end of the Shiva lingam?"

"No, I didn't." I travelled on and on, but I couldn't find the end, so I returned here. Did you find the end?"

"Well, yes, in fact, I did. I went right up to the top of the Shiva lingam, where I took the Darshan of the divine Lord Shiva, and then I came back down to tell you."

"What kind of story are you telling me?" replied Vishnu in disbelief. How could you find the end of the Shiva lingam? There was no end down below. How could there be an end on top? What proof do you have?"

Brahma said, "I thought you might not believe me, so I brought this little flower from the top of the Shiva lingam to testify on my behalf. Ask this flower. I brought him down from Lord Shiva's head just to show you."

Vishnu looked at the flower and asked, "Flower, is that correct? Did you really come from the head of Lord Shiva?"

"Oh yes, Vishnu," replied the little flower. "I really came from the top of Lord Shiva's head."

"Did Brahma take you from the top of Lord Shiva's head?" Vishnu questioned again.

The poor little flower began to shake. "Ye-ye-ye-yes, Vishnu. Brahma took me from the top of Shiva's head just to show you that he was there."

Suddenly the earth began to shake. The clouds broke apart, and through the four regions of heaven came the roaring sound, "LIAR!"

Shiva came down and said, "No one came to the top of that lingam, and nobody took that flower off from my head. Brahma, you are a LIAR! And this flower is lying. It is not possible to reach to the summit of infinity without my Grace. Knowledge of the Self is not an attainment. It is a realization of Being in the present reality. Realization comes about through intuitive awareness, not through egotistical action. If you want to earn that Grace, then refine and purify your awareness through selfless actions. Perform the worship of my Shiva lingam, the eternal symbol of the Consciousness of Infinite Goodness, and being pleased I will grant to you that vision. There is no other way to attainment."

ॐ सदा शिवाय विद्महे सहस्राक्षाय धीमहे ।

तन्नो शम्भो प्रचोदयात् ॥

ওঁ সদা শিবায় বিধ্মহে সহশ্রাক্ষায় ধীমহে ।

তন্নো শম্ভো প্রচোদয়াত ।।

oṃ sadā śivāya vidhmahe sahaśrākṣāya dhīmahe |
tanno śambho pracodayāt ||

oṃ We meditate upon the Perfect, Full, Complete, Always Continuing, Consciousness of Infinite Goodness; contemplate He Whose Thousand Eyes see everywhere. May that Giver of Bliss grant us increase.

(Wave light)

ॐ अग्नि ज्योति रवि ज्योतिष्चन्द्र ज्योतिष्तथैव च ।

ज्योतिशमुत्तमो देव दीपोऽयं प्रतिगृह्यतम् ॥

एष दीपः ॐ नमः शिवाय

ওঁ অগ্নি জ্যোতি রবি জ্যোতিষ্চন্দ্র জ্যোতিষ্তথৈব চ ।

জ্যোতিশমুত্তমো দেব দীপোহয়ং প্রতিগৃহ্যতম্ ।।

এষ দীপঃ ওঁ নমঃ শিবায়

oṃ agni jyoti ravi jyotiṣ candra jyotiṣ tathaiva ca |
jyoti śamuttamo deva dīpo-yaṃ pratigṛhyatam ||
eṣa dīpaḥ oṃ namaḥ śivāya

oṃ The Divine Fire is the Light, the Light of Wisdom is the Light, the Light of Devotion is the Light as well. The Light of the Highest Bliss, Oh Lord, is in the Light which I offer, the Light which I request you to accept. With the offering of Light oṃ We bow to The Consciousness of Infinite Goodness.

(Wave incense)

ॐ वनस्पतिरसोत्पन्नो गन्ध्यात्येया गन्ध्य उत्तमः ।

आघ्रेयः सर्व देवानां धूपोऽयं प्रतिगृह्यतम् ॥

एष धूपः ॐ नमः शिवाय

ওঁ বনস্পতিরসোত্পন্নো গন্ধ্যাত্যেয়া গন্ধ্য উত্তমঃ ।

আঘ্রেয়ঃ সর্ব দেবানাং ধূপোহয়ং প্রতিগৃহ্যতম্ ।।

এষ ধূপঃ ওঁ নমঃ শিবায়

oṃ vanaspatirasotpanno gandhyātyeyā gandhya uttamaḥ |
āghreyaḥ sarva devānāṃ dhūpo-yaṃ pratigṛhyatam ||
eṣa dhūpaḥ oṃ namaḥ śivāya

oṃ Spirit of the Forest, from you is produced the most excellent of scents. The scent most pleasing to all the Gods, that scent I request you to accept. With the offering of fragrant scent oṃ We bow to The Consciousness of Infinite Goodness.

(Folded hands)

ॐ भूर्भुवः स्वः । तत् सवितुर्वरेण्यम् भर्गो देवस्य धीमहि ।

धियो यो नः प्रचोदयात् ॥

ওঁ ভূর্ভুবঃ স্বঃ । তত্ সবিতুর্বরেণ্যম্ ভর্গো দেবস্য

ধীমহি । ধিয়ো য়ো নঃ প্রচোদয়াত্ ।।

oṃ bhūr bhuvaḥ svaḥ | tat savitur vareṇyam bhargo devasya dhīmahi | dhiyo yo naḥ pracodayāt ||

Oṃ the Infinite Beyond Conception, the gross body, the subtle body and the causal body; we meditate upon that Light of Wisdom which is the Supreme Wealth of the Gods. May it grant to us increase in our meditations.

Offer a flower with each mantra ete gandhapuṣpe

एते गन्धपुष्पे ॐ गँ गणपतये नमः

এতে গন্ধপুষ্পে ওঁ গঁ গণপতয়ে নমঃ

ete gandhapuṣpe oṃ gaṁ gaṇapataye namaḥ

With these scented flowers oṃ I bow to the Lord of Wisdom, Lord of the Multitudes.

एते गन्धपुष्पे ॐ अदित्यादि नवग्रहेभ्यो नमः

এতে গন্ধপুষ্পে ওঁ আদিত্যাদি নবগ্রহেভ্যো নমঃ

ete gandhapuṣpe oṃ ādityādi navagrahebhyo namaḥ

With these scented flowers oṃ I bow to the Sun, the Light of Wisdom, along with the nine planets.

एते गन्धपुष्पे ॐ शिवादिपञ्चदेवताभ्यो नमः

এতে গন্ধপুষ্পে ওঁ শিবাদিপঞ্চদেবতাভ্যো নমঃ

ete gandhapuṣpe oṃ śivādipañcadevatābhyo namaḥ

With these scented flowers oṃ I bow to Śiva, the Consciousness of Infinite Goodness, along with the five primary deities (Śiva, Śakti, Viṣṇu, Gaṇeṣa, Sūrya).

एते गन्धपुष्पे ॐ इन्द्रादिदशदिक्पालेभ्यो नमः

এতে গন্ধপুষ্পে ওঁ ইন্দ্রাদিদশদিক্পালেভ্যো নমঃ

ete gandhapuṣpe oṃ indrādi daśa dikpālebhyo namaḥ

With these scented flowers oṃ I bow to Indra, the Ruler of the Pure, along with the Ten Protectors of the ten directions.

एते गन्धपुष्पे ॐ मत्स्यादिदशावतारेभ्यो नमः

এতে গন্ধপুষ্পে ওঁ মৎস্যাদিদশাবতারেভ্যো নমঃ

ete gandhapuṣpe oṃ matsyādi daśāvatārebhyo namaḥ

With these scented flowers oṃ I bow to Vishnu, the Fish, along with the Ten Incarnations which He assumed.

एते गन्धपुष्पे ॐ प्रजापतये नमः

এতে গন্ধপুষ্পে ওঁ প্রজাপতয়ে নমঃ

ete gandhapuṣpe oṃ prajāpataye namaḥ

With these scented flowers oṃ I bow to the Lord of All Created Beings.

एते गन्धपुष्पे ॐ नमो नारायणाय नमः

এতে গন্ধপুষ্পে ওঁ নমো নারায়ণায় নমঃ

ete gandhapuṣpe oṃ namo nārāyaṇāya namaḥ

With these scented flowers oṃ I bow to the Perfect Perception of Consciousness.

एते गन्धपुष्पे ॐ सर्वेभ्यो देवेभ्यो नमः

এতে গন্ধপুষ্পে ওঁ সর্বেভ্যো দেবেভ্যো নমঃ

ete gandhapuṣpe oṃ sarvebhyo devebhyo namaḥ

With these scented flowers oṃ I bow to All the Gods.

एते गन्धपुष्पे ॐ सर्वाभ्यो देवीभ्यो नमः

এতে গন্ধপুষ্পে ওঁ সর্বাভ্যো দেবীভ্যো নমঃ

ete gandhapuṣpe oṃ sarvābhyo devībhyo namaḥ

With these scented flowers oṃ I bow to All the Goddesses.

एते गन्धपुष्पे ॐ श्री गुरवे नमः

এতে গন্ধপুষ্পে ওঁ শ্রী গুরবে নমঃ

ete gandhapuṣpe oṃ śrī gurave namaḥ

With these scented flowers oṃ I bow to the Respected Guru.

एते गन्धपुष्पे ॐ ब्राह्मणेभ्यो नमः

এতে গন্ধপুষ্পে ওঁ ব্রাহ্মণেভ্যো নমঃ

ete gandhapuṣpe oṃ brāhmaṇebhyo namaḥ

With these scented flowers oṃ I bow to All Knowers of Wisdom.

ĀCHAMAN

Pour some water in right palm. Sip some water after each oṃ viṣṇu, then clean hands with remaining water and dry

ॐ विष्णु ॐ विष्णु ॐ विष्णु

ওঁ বিষ্ণু ওঁ বিষ্ণু ওঁ বিষ্ণু

oṃ viṣṇu oṃ viṣṇu oṃ viṣṇu

oṃ Consciousness, oṃ Consciousness, oṃ Consciousness

Draw the following yantra with some drops of water and/or sandal paste at the front of your seat. Place a flower on the bindu in the middle.

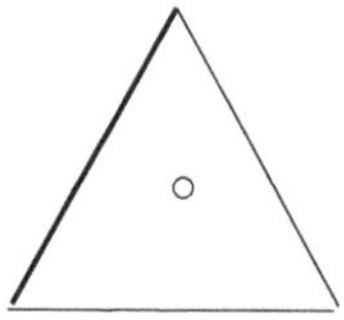

एते गन्धपुष्पे ॐ ह्रीं आधारशक्तये

कमलासनाय नमः ॥

এতে গন্ধপুষ্পে ওঁ হ্রীঁ আধারশক্তয়ে

কমলাসনায় নমঃ।।

ete gandhapuṣpe oṃ hrīṃ ādhāra śaktaye kamalāsanāya namaḥ

With these scented flowers oṃ hrīṃ I bow to the Primal Energy situated in this lotus seat.

Clap hands 3 times and snap fingers in the ten directions (N S E W NE SW NW SE UP DOWN) repeating oṃ namaḥ śivāya.

ॐ नमः शिवाय

ওঁ নমঃ শিবায়

oṃ namaḥ śivāya

oṃ I bow to the Consciousness of Infinite Goodness.

शिव पूजा Śiva Pūjā শিব পূজা

Place a flower in left hand. Pour 3 drops of water on it after oṃ tat sat. *Place right hand over flower and finish reciting this verse with the appropriate names added (refer to a lunar calendar, if available), then offer the flower.*

विष्णुः ॐ तत् सत् । ॐ अद्य जम्बूद्वीपे ( ) देश ( ) प्रदेश

( ) नगरे ( ) मन्दिरे ( ) मासे ( ) पक्षे ( ) तिथौ

( ) गोत्र श्री ( ) कृतैतत् श्री शिव कामः पूजा कर्माहं करिष्ये ॥

বিষ্ণুঃ ওঁ তত্ সত্ । ওঁ অদ্য জম্বূদ্বীপে ( ) দেশে

( ) প্রদেশে ( ) নগরে ( ) মন্দিরে ( ) মাসে

( ) পক্ষে ( ) তিথৌ ( ) গোত্র, শ্রী

( ) কৃতৈতত্ শ্রী শিব কামঃ পূজা কর্মাহং করিষ্যে ।।

viṣṇuḥ oṃ tat sat । oṃ adya jambūdvīpe, (Country) deśe, (state) pradeśe, (City) nagare, (Divine Mother) mandire, (month) māse, (śukla or krişṇa) pakṣe, (name of day) tithau, {name of (Satyānanda)} gotra, śrī (your name) kṛtaitat, śrī śiva kāmaḥ, pūjā karmāham kariṣye

The Consciousness Which Pervades All, oṃ That is Truth. Presently, on the Planet Earth, (America) Country, (Name) State, (Name) City, in (Devi Mandir) Temple, (Name of Month) Month, (Bright or Dark) fortnight, (Name of Day) Day, Name of Sadhu Family (Satyānanda) Gotra, Śrī (Your Name) is performing for the satisfaction of Śiva, the Consciousness of Infinite Goodness.

Ring Bell

ॐ शान्ता द्यौ शान्ता पृथिवीं, शान्तमूर्ध्वमूर्वन्तरिक्षम् ।

शान्तमूध्वम्वतिरापः शान्तां नः शान्त्वोषधी ॥

ওঁ শান্তা দ্যৌ শান্তা পৃথিবীং, শান্তমূর্ধ্বমূর্বন্তরিক্ষম্ ।

শান্তমূর্ধ্বম্বতিরাপঃ শান্তাং নঃ শান্ত্বোষধী ।।

oṃ śāntā dyau śāntā pṛthivīṃ, śāntam ūrdhvam ūrvantarikṣam śāntam ūrdhvam vatirāpaḥ śāntāṃ naḥ śāntvoṣadhī

Peace in the heavens, Peace on the earth, Peace upwards and permeating the atmosphere; Peace upwards, over, on all sides and further; Peace to us, Peace to all vegetation;

शान्तानि पूर्वरूपाणि शान्तं नोऽस्तु कृताकृतम् ।
शान्तं भूतं च भव्यं च सर्वमेव समस्तु नः ॥

শান্তাণি পূর্বরূপাণি শান্তং নোহস্তু কৃতাকৃতম্ ।
শান্তং ভূতং চ ভব্যং চ সর্বমেব সমস্তু নঃ ।।

śāntāṇi pūrva rūpāṇi śāntaṃ no-stu kṛtā kṛtam
śāntaṃ bhūtaṃ ca bhavyaṃ ca sarvameva samastu naḥ

Peace to all that has form, Peace to all causes and effects; Peace to all existence, and to all intensities of reality including all and everything; Peace be to us.

पृथिवीं शान्तिरन्तरिक्षं शान्तिर्द्यौ । शान्तिरापः, शान्तिरोषधयः, शान्तिः वनस्पतयः, शान्तिर्विश्वे मे देवाः, शान्तिः सर्व मे देवाः, शान्तिर्ब्रह्म, शान्तिरापः, शान्ति सर्वम्, शान्तिरेधि, शान्तिः, शान्तिः, सर्व शान्ति, सा मा शान्ति, शान्तिभिः ॥

পৃথিবীং শান্তিরন্তরিক্ষং শন্তির্দ্যৌ । শান্তিরাপঃ, শান্তিরোষধয়ঃ, শান্তিঃ বনস্পতয়ঃ, শান্তির্বিশ্বে মে দেবাঃ, শান্তিঃ সর্ব মে দেবাঃ, শান্তির্ব্রহ্ম, শান্তিরাপঃ, শান্তি সর্বম্ শান্তিরেধি, শান্তিঃ, শান্তিঃ, সর্ব শান্তি, সা মা শান্তি, শান্তিভিঃ ।।

pṛthivīṃ śāntir antarikṣaṃ śāntir dyau
śāntir āpaḥ, śāntir oṣadayaḥ, śāntiḥ vanaspatayaḥ, śāntir viśve me devāḥ, śāntiḥ sarva me devāḥ, śāntir brahma, śāntirāpaḥ, śānti sarvam, śāntiredhi, śāntiḥ, śāntiḥ, sarva śānti, sā mā śānti, śāntibhiḥ

Let the earth be at Peace, the atmosphere be at Peace, the heavens be filled with Peace. Even further may Peace extend,

Peace to all vegetation, Peace to All Gods of the Universe, Peace to All Gods within me, Peace to Creative Consciousness, Peace be to Brilliant Light, Peace to All, Peace to Everything, Peace, Peace, altogether Peace, equally Peace, by means of Peace.

ॐ शान्तिः, शान्तिः, शान्तिः

ওঁ শান্তিঃ, শান্তিঃ, শান্তিঃ

oṃ śāntiḥ, śāntiḥ, śāntiḥ

Peace, Peace, Peace

Draw the following yantra near the lingam on the plate, or space for worship with sandal paste and/or water. Offer rice on the yantra for each of the next four mantras.

ॐ आधारशक्तये नमः

ওঁ আধারশক্তয়ে নমঃ

oṃ ādhāra śaktaye namaḥ

oṃ I bow to the Primal Energy

ॐ कुर्म्माय नमः

ওঁ কূর্ম্মায় নমঃ

oṃ kurmmāya namaḥ

oṃ I bow to the Support of the Earth

ॐ अनन्ताय नमः

ওঁ অনন্তায় নমঃ

oṃ anantāya namaḥ

oṃ I bow to Infinity

ॐ पृथिव्यै नमः

ওঁ পৃথিব্যৈ নমঃ

oṃ pṛthivyai namaḥ

oṃ I bow to the Earth

Place an empty water pot on the bindu in the center of the yantra when saying **phaṭ**

स्थां स्थीं स्थीरो भव फट्

স্থাং স্থীং স্থীরো ভব ফট্

sthāṃ sthīṃ sthīro bhava phaṭ

Be Still in the Gross Body! Be Still in the Subtle Body! Be Still in the Causal Body! PURIFY!

Fill pot with water while chanting mantra.

ॐ गङ्गे च जमुने चैव गोदावरि सरस्वति ।

नर्मदे सिन्धुकावेरि जलेहस्मिन् सन्निधिं कुरु ॥

ওঁ গঙ্গে চ যমনে চৈব গোদাবরি সরস্বতি ।

নর্মদে সিন্ধুকাবেরি জলেহস্মিন্ সন্নিধিং কুরু ।।

oṃ gaṅge ca jamune caiva godāvari sarasvati
narmade sindhu kāveri jalehasmin sannidhiṃ kuru

oṃ the Ganges, Jamuna, Godāvari, Saraswati, Narmada, Sindhu, Kāveri these waters are mingled together.

Note. The Ganges is the Iḍa, Jamuna is the Pingalā. The other five rivers are the five senses. The land of the seven rivers is within the body as well as outside.

Offer 3 flowers into the water pot with the mantra

एते गन्धपुष्पे ॐ नमः शिवाय

এতে গন্ধপুষ্পে ওঁ নমঃ শিবায়

ete gandhapuṣpe oṃ namaḥ śivāya

With these scented flowers oṃ I bow to the Consciousness of Infinite Goodness.

Wave right hand in aṅkuṣa mudrā while chanting this mantra.

ॐ गङ्गे च जमुने चैव गोदावरि सरस्वति ।

नर्मदे सिन्धुकावेरि जलेहस्मिन् सन्निधिं कुरु ॥

ওঁ গঙ্গে চ যমুনে চৈব গোদাবরি সরস্বতি ।

নর্মদে সিন্ধুকাবেরি জলেহস্মিন্ সন্নিধিং কুরু ।।

oṃ gaṅge ca jamune caiva godāvari sarasvati
narmade sindhu kāveri jalehasmin sannidhiṃ kuru

oṃ the Ganges, Jamuna, Godāvari, Saraswati, Narmada, Sindhu, Kāveri these waters are mingled together.

ॐ नमः शिवाय 10 times

ওঁ নমঃ শিবায়

oṃ namaḥ śivāya

oṃ I bow to the Consciousness of Infinite Goodness.

Sprinkle water over all articles to be offered, then throw some drops of water over your shoulders repeating the mantra:

अमृताम् कुरु स्वाहा

অমৃতাম্ কুরু স্বাহা

amritām kuru svāhā

Make this immortal nectar! I am One with God!

puṣpa śuddhi

Wave hands over flowers with prarthana mudrā while chanting first line and with dhenu mudrā while chanting second line of this mantra.

ॐ पुष्प पुष्प महापुष्प सुपुष्प पुष्पसम्भवे ।

पुष्प चयावकीर्णे च हूं फट् स्वाहा ॥

ওঁ পুষ্প পুষ্প মহাপুষ্প সুপুষ্প পুষ্পসম্ভবে ।

পুষ্প চয়াবকীর্ণে চ হূং ফট্ স্বাহা ।।

oṃ puṣpa puṣpa mahā puṣpa supuṣpa puṣpasambhave
puṣpa cayāvakīrṇe ca hūṃ phaṭ svāhā

oṃ Flowers, flowers, Oh Great Flowers, excellent flowers; flowers in heaps and scattered about, cut the ego, purify, I am One with God!

Offer a flower while chanting each of the following mantras ete gandhapuṣpe

एते गन्धपुष्पे ॐ ह्रीं चण्डिकायै नमः

এতে গন্ধপুষ্পে ওঁ হ্রীঁ চণ্ডিকায়ৈ নমঃ

ete gandhapuṣpe oṃ hrīṃ caṇḍikāyai namaḥ

With these scented flowers oṃ I bow to She Who Tears Apart Thought

एते गन्धपुष्पे ॐ ह्रीं श्रीं दुं दुर्गायै नमः

এতে গন্ধপুষ্পে ওঁ হ্রীঁ শ্রীঁ দুং দুর্গায়ৈ নমঃ

ete gandhapuṣpe oṃ hrīṃ śrīṃ duṃ durgāyai namaḥ

With these scented flowers oṃ I bow to the Reliever of Difficulties

एते गन्धपुष्पे ॐ क्रीं काल्यै नमः

এতে গন্ধপুষ্পে ওঁ ক্রীঁ কাল্যৈ নমঃ

ete gandhapuṣpe oṃ krīṃ kālyai namaḥ

With these scented flowers oṃ I bow to the She Who Is Beyond Time (also the Goddess Who Takes Away Darkness)

एते गन्धपुष्पे ॐ श्रीं लक्ष्मयै नमः

এতে গন্ধপুষ্পে ওঁ শ্রীঁ লক্ষ্ম্যৈ নমঃ

ete gandhapuṣpe oṃ śrīṃ lakṣmyai namaḥ

With these scented flowers oṃ I bow to the Goddess of True Wealth

एते गन्धपुष्पे ॐ सं सरस्वत्यै नमः

এতে গন্ধপুষ্পে ওঁ সং সরস্বত্যৈ নমঃ

ete gandhapuṣpe oṃ saṃ sarasvatyai namaḥ

With these scented flowers oṃ I bow to the Spirit of All-Pervading Knowledge

एते गन्धपुष्पे ॐ बौं ब्रह्मणे नमः

এতে গন্ধপুষ্পে ওঁ বৌং ব্রহ্মণে নমঃ

ete gandhapuṣpe oṃ bauṃ brahmaṇe namaḥ

With these scented flowers oṃ I bow to the Creative Consciousness

एते गन्धपुष्पे ॐ क्लीं विष्णवे नमः

এতে গন্ধপুষ্পে ওঁ ক্লীঁ বিষ্ণবে নমঃ

ete gandhapuṣpe oṃ klīṃ viṣṇave namaḥ

With these scented flowers oṃ I bow to the Consciousness Which Pervades All

एते गन्धपुष्पे ॐ नमः शिवाय

এতে গন্ধপুষ্পে ওঁ নমঃ শিবায়

ete gandhapuṣpe oṃ namaḥ śivāya

With these scented flowers oṃ I bow to the Consciousness of Infinite Goodness

एते गन्धपुष्पे ॐ हराय नमः

এতে গন্ধপুষ্পে ওঁ হরায় নমঃ

ete gandhapuṣpe oṃ harāya namaḥ

With these scented flowers oṃ I bow to He Who Takes Away

एते गन्धपुष्पे ॐ महेश्वराय नमः

এতে গন্ধপুষ্পে ওঁ মহেশ্বরায় নমঃ

ete gandhapuṣpe oṃ maheśvarāya namaḥ

With these scented flowers oṃ I bow to the Great Lord of All, or Great Seer of All

Dhyānam

Place a flower in your left hand, cover it with the right hand while reciting this mantra.Then offer flower

ॐ ध्यायेन्नित्यं महेशं रजतगिरिनिभं चारुचन्द्रावतंसं
रत्ना कल्पोज्वलाण्गं परशु मृगवयाभीति हस्तं प्रसन्नं ।
पद्मासीनं समन्तात् स्तुतऽममरगणैव्याघ्रकृत्तिं वसानं
विश्वाद्यं विश्वबीजं निखलभयहरं पञ्चवक्त्रं त्रिनेत्रं ॥

ওঁ ধ্যায়েন্নিত্যং মহেশং রজতগিরিনিভং চারুচন্দ্রাবতংসং
রত্না কল্পোজ্বলাঙ্গং পরশু মৃগবয়াভীতি হস্তং প্রসন্নং ।
পদ্মাসীনং সমন্তাৎ স্তুতহমমরগণৈর্ব্যঘ্রকৃত্তিং বসানং
বিশ্বাদ্যং বিশ্ববীজং নিখলভয়হরং পঞ্চবক্ত্রং ত্রিনেত্রং ।।

oṃ dhyāyen nityaṃ maheśaṃ
rajata girinibhaṃ cāru candrā vataṃsaṃ
ratnā kalpo jvalāṇgaṃ
paraśu mṛga vayābhīti hastaṃ prasannaṃ
padmāsīnaṃ samantāt
stuta-mama raganair vyāghra kṛtiṃ vasānaṃ
viśvādyaṃ viśva bījaṃ
nikhala bhayaharaṃ pañca vaktraṃ trinetraṃ

We always meditate on He who shines like the white mountains, ornamented by a digit of the moon on His head. His body shines like jewels. In His left hands He displays an axe and the mṛga mudrā (kalpataru mudrā, with the thumb, middle and ring fingers joined with the pointer and pinky extended up) and in His two right hands He shows mudrās granting blessings and fearlessness. He is of beautiful appearance seated in the full lotus asana. On His four sides the Gods are present singing hymns of praise. His wearing apparel is a tiger's skin. He is before the universe and the cause of the universe. He removes all fear, has five faces and three eyes.

ॐ नं अंगुष्ठाभ्यां नमः

ওঁ নং অঙ্গুষ্ঠাভ্যাং নমঃ

oṃ naṃ aṅguṣṭhābhyāṃ namaḥ *thumb/forefinger*

oṃ naṃ in the thumb I bow.

ॐ मः तर्जनीभ्यां स्वाहा

ওঁ মঃ তর্জনীভ্যাং স্বাহা

oṃ maḥ tarjanībhyāṃ svāhā *thumb/forefinger*

oṃ maḥ in the forefinger, I am One with God!

ॐ शिं मध्यमाभ्यां वषट्

ওঁ শিং মধ্যমাভ্যাং বষট্

oṃ śiṃ madhyamābhyāṃ vaṣaṭ *thumb/middle finger*

oṃ śiṃ in the middle finger, Purify!

ॐ वां अनामिकाभ्यां हुं

ওঁ বাং অনামিকাভ্যাং হুং

oṃ vāṃ anāmikābhyāṃ huṃ *thumb/ring finger*

oṃ vāṃ in the ring finger, Cut the Ego!

ॐ यः कनिष्ठिकाभ्यां बौषट्

ওঁ য়ঃ কনিষ্ঠিকাভ্যাং বৌষট্

oṃ yaḥ kaniṣṭhikābhyāṃ vauṣaṭ *thumb/little finger*
oṃ yaḥ in the little finger, Ultimate Purity!

Roll hand over hand forwards while reciting karatala kara, *and backwards while chanting* pṛṣṭhābhyāṃ, *then clap hands when chanting* astrāya phaṭ

ॐ नमः शिवाय करतल कर पृष्ठाभ्यां अस्त्राय फट् ॥

ওঁ নমঃ শিবায় করতল কর পৃষ্ঠাভ্যাং অস্ত্রায় ফট্ ।।

oṃ namaḥ śivāya karatala kara pṛṣṭhābhyāṃ astrāya phaṭ
oṃ I bow to the Consciousness of Infinite Goodness with the weapon of Virtue.

ॐ नमः शिवाय

ওঁ নমঃ শিবায়

oṃ namaḥ śivāya
I bow to the Consciousness of Infinite Goodness.

Holding tattwa mudrā, touch heart.

ॐ नं हृदयाय नमः

ওঁ নং হৃদয়ায় নমঃ

oṃ naṃ hṛdayāya namaḥ *touch heart*
oṃ naṃ in the heart, I bow.

Holding tattwa mudrā, touch top of head.

ॐ मः शिरसे स्वाहा

ওঁ মঃ শিরসে স্বাহা

oṃ maḥ śirase svāhā *top of head*
oṃ maḥ on the top of the head, I am One with God!

शिव पूजा Śiva Pūjā শিব পূজা

With thumb extended, touch back of head.

ॐ शिं शिखायै वषट्

ওঁ শিং শিখায়ৈ বষট্

oṃ śiṃ śikhāyai vaṣaṭ *back of head*

oṃ śiṃ on the back of the head, Purify!

Holding tattwa mudrā, cross both arms.

ॐ वां कवचाय हुं

ওঁ বাং কবচায় হুং

oṃ vāṃ kavacāya huṃ *cross both arms*

oṃ vāṃ crossing both arms, Cut the Ego!

Holding tattwa mudrā, touch three eyes at once with three middle fingers.

ॐ यः नेत्रत्रयाय वौषट्

ওঁ য়ঃ নেত্রত্রয়ায় বৌষট্

oṃ yaḥ netratrayāya vauṣaṭ *touch three eyes*

oṃ yaḥ in the three eyes, Ultimate Purity!

Roll hand over hand forwards while reciting karatala kara, *and backwards while chanting* pṛṣṭhābhyāṃ, *then clap hands when chanting* astrāya phaṭ .

ॐ नमः शिवाय करतल कर पृष्ठाभ्यां अस्त्राय फट् ॥

ওঁ নমঃ শিবায় করতল কর পৃষ্ঠাভ্যাং অস্ত্রায় ফট্ ।।

oṃ namaḥ śivāya karatala kara pṛṣṭhābhyāṃ astrāya phaṭ

oṃ I bow to the Consciousness of Infinite Goodness with the weapon of Virtue.

शिव पूजा Śiva Pūjā শিব পূজা

ॐ नमः शिवाय

ওঁ নমঃ শিবায়

oṃ namaḥ śivāya
I bow to the Consciousness of Infinite Goodness.

ॐ नमः शिवाय

ওঁ নমঃ শিবায়

oṃ namaḥ śivāya (108 times)
I bow to the Consciousness of Infinite Goodness.

If desired, collect the next eight liquid offerings in a bowl or offer them directly to the lingam.

foot bath

ॐ नमः शिवाय पाद्यं समर्पयामि ॥

ওঁ নমঃ শিবায় পাদ্যং সমর্পয়ামি ।।

oṃ namaḥ śivāya pādyaṃ samarpayāmi
oṃ We bow to The Consciousness of Infinite Goodness and offer these foot bath waters.

milk bath

ॐ नमः शिवाय पयः स्नानं समर्पयामि ॥

ওঁ নমঃ শিবায় পয়ঃ স্নানং সমর্পয়ামি ।।

oṃ namaḥ śivāya payaḥ snānaṃ samarpayāmi
oṃ We bow to The Consciousness of Infinite Goodness and offer this milk for your bath.

yogurt bath

ॐ नमः शिवाय दधि स्नानं समर्पयामि ॥

ওঁ নমঃ শিবায় দধি স্নানং সমর্পয়ামি ।।

oṃ namaḥ śivāya dadhi snānaṃ samarpayāmi
oṃ We bow to The Consciousness of Infinite Goodness and offer this curd for your bath.

ghee bath

ॐ नमः शिवाय घृत स्नानं समर्पयामि ॥

ওঁ নমঃ শিবায় ঘৃত স্নানং সমর্পয়ামি ।।

oṃ namaḥ śivāya ghṛta snānaṃ samarpayāmi

oṃ We bow to The Consciousness of Infinite Goodness and offer this ghee for your bath.

honey bath

ॐ नमः शिवाय मधु स्नानं समर्पयामि ॥

ওঁ নমঃ শিবায় মধু স্নানং সমর্পয়ামি ।।

oṃ namaḥ śivāya madhu snānaṃ samarpayāmi

oṃ We bow to The Consciousness of Infinite Goodness and offer this honey for your bath.

sugar bath

ॐ नमः शिवाय शर्करा स्नानं समर्पयामि ॥

ওঁ নমঃ শিবায় শর্করা স্নানং সমর্পয়ামি ।।

oṃ namaḥ śivāya śarkarā snānaṃ samarpayāmi

oṃ We bow to The Consciousness of Infinite Goodness and offer this sugar for your bath.

five nectars bath

ॐ नमः शिवाय पञ्चामृतं स्नानं समर्पयामि ॥

ওঁ নমঃ শিবায় পঞ্চামৃতং স্নানং সমর্পয়ামি ।।

oṃ namaḥ śivāya pañcāmṛtaṃ snānaṃ samarpayāmi

oṃ We bow to The Consciousness of Infinite Goodness and offer these five nectars for your bath.

water bath

ॐ नमः शिवाय गङ्गा स्नानं समर्पयामि ॥

ওঁ নমঃ শিবায় গঙ্গা স্নানং সমর্পয়ামি ।।

oṃ namaḥ śivāya gaṇgā snānaṃ samarpayāmi

oṃ We bow to The Consciousness of Infinite Goodness and offer these bath waters.

cloth

ॐ नमः शिवाय वस्त्रां समर्पयामि ॥

ওঁ নমঃ শিবায় বস্ত্রাং সমর্পয়ামি ।।

oṃ namaḥ śivāya vastrāṃ samarpayāmi

oṃ We bow to The Consciousness of Infinite Goodness and offer this wearing aparell.

rudrākṣa

ॐ नमः शिवाय रुद्राक्षं समर्पयामि ॥

ওঁ নমঃ শিবায় রুদ্রাক্ষং সমর্পয়ামি ।।

oṃ namaḥ śivāya rudrākṣaṃ samarpayāmi

oṃ We bow to The Consciousness of Infinite Goodness and offer this rudrākṣa.

red powder

ॐ नमः शिवाय सिन्दूरं समर्पयामि ॥

ওঁ নমঃ শিবায় সিন্দূরং সমর্পয়ামি ।।

oṃ namaḥ śivāya sindūraṃ samarpayāmi

oṃ We bow to The Consciousness of Infinite Goodness and offer this red colored powder.

sandal paste

ॐ नमः शिवाय चन्दनं समर्पयामि ॥

ওঁ নমঃ শিবায় চন্দনং সমর্পয়ামি ।।

oṃ namaḥ śivāya candanaṃ samarpayāmi

oṃ We bow to The Consciousness of Infinite Goodness and offer this sandal paste.

rice

ॐ नमः शिवाय अक्षतं समर्पयामि ॥

ওঁ নমঃ শিবায় অক্ষতং সমর্পয়ামি ।।

oṃ namaḥ śivāya akṣataṃ samarpayāmi

oṃ We bow to The Consciousness of Infinite Goodness and offer these grains of rice.

flower garland

ॐ नमः शिवाय पुष्पमालां समर्पयामि ॥

ওঁ নমঃ শিবায় পুষ্পমালাং সমর্পয়ামি ।।

oṃ namaḥ śivāya puṣpamālāṃ samārpāyāmi

oṃ We bow to The Consciousness of Infinite Goodness and offer this garland of flowers .

food offering

ॐ नमः शिवाय भोग नैवेद्यम् समर्पयामि ॥

ওঁ নমঃ শিবায় ভোগ নৈবেদ্যম্ সমর্পয়ামি ।।

oṃ namaḥ śivāya bhog naivedyam samarpayāmi

oṃ We bow to The Consciousness of Infinite Goodness and offer this presentation of food.

drinking water

ॐ नमः शिवाय पानार्थ जलम् समर्पयामि ॥

ওঁ নমঃ শিবায় পানার্থ জলম্ সমর্পয়ামি ।।

oṃ namaḥ śivāya pānārtha jalam samarpayāmi

oṃ We bow to The Consciousness of Infinite Goodness and offer this drinking water.

एते गन्धपुष्पे ॐ नमः शिवाय

এতে গন্ধপুষ্পে ওঁ নমঃ শিবায়

ete gandha puṣpe oṃ namaḥ śivāya

With these scented flowers oṃ We bow to the Consciousness of Infinite Goodness

ॐ नमः शिवाय

ওঁ নমঃ শিবায়

oṃ namaḥ śivāya (108 times)

oṃ I bow to the Consciousness of Infinite Goodness

- 1 -

ॐ शिवाय नमः

ওঁ শিবায় নমঃ

Oṃ Śivāya namaḥ

Oṃ we bow to the Consciousness of Infinite Goodness.

- 2 -

ॐ महेश्वराय नमः

ওঁ মহেশ্বরায় নমঃ

Oṃ Maheśvarāya namaḥ

Oṃ we bow to the great seer of all.

- 3 -

ॐ शम्भवे नमः

ওঁ শম্ভবে নমঃ

Oṃ Śambhave namaḥ

Oṃ we bow to he whose reality is peace.

- 4 -

ॐ पिनाकिने नमः

ওঁ পিনাকিনে নমঃ

Oṃ Pinākine namaḥ

Oṃ we bow to he who holds the trident.

- 5 -

ॐ शशिशेखराय नमः

ওঁ শশিশেখরায় নমঃ

Oṃ Śaśiśekharāya namaḥ

Oṃ we bow to he upon whose head resides the moon.

- 6 -

ॐ वामदेवाय नमः

ওঁ বামদেবায় নমঃ

Oṃ Vāmadevāya namaḥ

Oṃ we bow the beautiful god of love.

-7 -

ॐ विरूपाक्षाय नमः

ওঁ বিরূপাক্ষায় নমঃ

Oṃ Virūpākṣāya namaḥ

Oṃ we bow to he whose eyes see beyond form.

- 8 -

ॐ कपर्दिने नमः

ওঁ কপর্দিনে নমঃ

Oṃ Kapardine namaḥ

Oṃ we bow to he who holds a head.

- 9 -

ॐ नीलल्लोहिताय नमः

ওঁ নীললোহিতায় নমঃ

Oṃ Nīlalohitāya namaḥ

Oṃ we bow to he who is red and blue.

- 10 -

ॐ शङ्कराय नमः

ওঁ শঙ্করায় নমঃ

Oṃ Śaṅkarāya namaḥ

Oṃ we bow to the cause of peace.

- 11 -

ॐ शूलपाणये नमः

ওঁ শূলপাণয়ে নমঃ

Oṃ Śūlapāṇaye namaḥ

Oṃ we bow to he with spear in hand.

- 12 -

ॐ खट्वांगिने नमः

ওঁ খট্বাংগিনে নমঃ

Oṃ Khaṭvāṃgine namaḥ

Oṃ we bow to he who holds a staff
(or missiles of consciousness).

- 13 -

ॐ विष्णुबल्लभाय नमः

ওঁ বিষ্ণুবল্লভায় নমঃ

Oṃ Visṇuballabhāya namaḥ

Oṃ we bow to the strength of Vishnu.

- 14 -

ॐ शिपिविष्टाय नमः

ওঁ শিপিবিষ্টায় নমঃ

Oṃ Śipiviṣṭāya namaḥ

Oṃ we bow to he who is present again and again.

- 15 -

ॐ अम्बिकानाथाय नमः

ওঁ অম্বিকানাথায় নমঃ

Oṃ Ambikānāthāya namaḥ

Oṃ we bow to the lord of the mother of the universe.

- 16 -

ॐ श्रीकण्ठाय नमः

ওঁ শ্রীকণ্ঠায় নমঃ

Oṃ Śrīkaṇṭhāya namaḥ

Oṃ we bow to he within whose throat
the Goddess of Respect dwells.

- 17-

ॐ भक्तवत्सलाय नमः

ওঁ ভক্তবৎসলায় নমঃ

Oṃ Bhaktavatsalāya namaḥ

Oṃ we bow to he who loves his devotees.

- 18 -

ॐ भवाय नमः

ওঁ ভবায় নমঃ

Oṃ Bhavāya namaḥ

Oṃ we bow to he who is the intensity of reality.

- 19 -

ॐ शर्वाय नमः

ওঁ শর্বায় নমঃ

Oṃ Śarvāya namaḥ

Oṃ we bow to he who is all.

- 20 -

ॐ त्रिलोकेशाय नमः

ওঁ ত্রিলোকেশায় নম

Oṃ Trilokeśāya namaḥ

Oṃ we bow to the ruler of the three worlds.

- 21 -

ॐ शितिकण्ठाय नमः

ওঁ শিতিকণ্ঠায় নমঃ

Oṃ Śitikaṇṭhāya namaḥ

Oṃ we bow to he who has a blue neck.

- 22 -

ॐ शिवाप्रियाय नमः

ওঁ শিবাপ্রিয়ায় নমঃ

Oṃ Śivāpriyāya namaḥ

Oṃ we bow to the beloved of the mother of the universe.

- 23 -

ॐ उग्राय नमः

ওঁ উগ্রায় নমঃ

Oṃ Ugrāya namaḥ

Oṃ we bow to he who is fierce.

- 24 -

ॐ कपालिने नमः

ওঁ কপালিনে নমঃ

Oṃ Kapāline namaḥ

Oṃ we bow to he who bears skulls.

- 25 -

ॐ कामरये नमः

ওঁ কামরয়ে নমঃ

Oṃ Kāmaraye namaḥ

Oṃ we bow to he who controls desire.

-26 -

ॐ महारूपाय नमः

ওঁ মহারূপায় নমঃ

Oṃ Mahārūpāya namaḥ

Oṃ we bow to he who is the great form.

-27 -

ॐ गङ्गाधराय नमः

ওঁ গঙ্গাধরায় নমঃ

Oṃ Gaṅgādharāya namaḥ

Oṃ we bow to he who supports the Ganges.

-28 -

ॐ ललाटाक्षाय नमः

ওঁ ললাটাক্ষায় নমঃ

Oṃ Lalāṭākṣāya namaḥ

Oṃ we bow to he whose third eye is visible on his forehead.

-29 -

ॐ कालकालाय नमः

ওঁ কালকালায় নমঃ

Oṃ Kālakālāya namaḥ

Oṃ we bow to he who is time after time.

- 30 -

ॐ कृपानिधये नमः

ওঁ কৃপানিধয়ে নমঃ

Oṃ Kṛpānidhaye namaḥ

Oṃ we bow to the giver of grace.

- 31 -

ॐ परशुहस्ताय नमः

ওঁ পরশুহস্তায় নমঃ

Oṃ Paraśuhastāya namaḥ

Oṃ we bow to he who has an axe in his hand.

- 32 -

ॐ मृगपाणये नमः

ওঁ মৃগপাণয়ে নমঃ

Oṃ Mṛgapāṇaye namaḥ

Oṃ we bow to he whose hand shows the mṛga mudrā.

- 33 -

ॐ जटाधराय नमः

ওঁ জটাধরায় নমঃ

Oṃ Jaṭādharāya namaḥ

Oṃ we bow to he who wears matted hair.

- 34 -

ॐ कैलासवासिने नमः

ওঁ কৈলাসবাসিনে নমঃ

Oṃ Kailāsavāsine namaḥ

Oṃ we bow to he who resides on Mount Kailash.

- 35 -

ॐ भीमाय नमः

ওঁ ভীমায় নমঃ

Oṃ Bhīmāya namaḥ

Oṃ we bow to he who is fearless.

- 36 -

ॐ कवचिने नमः

ওঁ কবচিনে নমঃ

Oṃ Kavacine namaḥ

Oṃ we bow to he who is an armor for protection.

- 37 -

ॐ कठोराय नमः

ওঁ কঠোরায় নমঃ

Oṃ Kaṭhorāya namaḥ

Oṃ we bow to he who is solid.

- 38 -

ॐ त्रिपूरान्तकाय नमः

ওঁ ত্রিপূরান্তকায় নমঃ

Oṃ Tripūrāntakāya namaḥ

Oṃ we bow to he who is the limit of the three cities.

- 39 -

ॐ वृषाङ्काय नमः

ওঁ বৃষাঙ্কায় নমঃ

Oṃ Vṛṣāṅkāya namaḥ

Oṃ we bow to he who travels with a bull.

- 40 -

ॐ वृषभारुढाय नमः

ওঁ বৃষভারুঢ়ায় নমঃ

Oṃ Vṛṣabhāruḍhāya namaḥ

Oṃ we bow to he who sits on a bull.

- 41 -

ॐ सर्वकर्मणे नमः

ওঁ সর্বকর্মণে নমঃ

Oṃ Sarvakarmaṇe namaḥ

Oṃ we bow to he who is all karma.

- 42 -

ॐ सामप्रियाय नमः

ওঁ সামপ্রিয়ায় নমঃ

Oṃ Sāmapriyāya namaḥ

Oṃ we bow to he who loves all songs.

- 43 -

ॐ स्वरम्याय नमः

ওঁ স্বরম্যায় নমঃ

Oṃ Svaramyāya namaḥ

Oṃ we bow to he whose praises are sung.

- 44 -

ॐ त्रिमूर्त्तये नमः

ওঁ ত্রিমূর্ত্তয়ে নমঃ

Oṃ Trimūrttaye namaḥ

Oṃ we bow to he who is three images of being.

- 45 -

ॐ सिद्धर्थाय नमः

ওঁ সিদ্ধর্থায় নমঃ

Oṃ Siddharthāya namaḥ

Oṃ we bow to he who is the object of perfection.

- 46 -

ॐ सर्वज्ञाय नमः

ওঁ সর্বজ্ঞায় নমঃ

Oṃ Sarvajñāya namaḥ

Oṃ we bow to he who is all wisdom.

- 47 -

ॐ परमात्मने नमः

ওঁ পরমাত্মনে নমঃ

Oṃ Paramātmane namaḥ

Oṃ we bow to he who is the supreme soul.

- 48 -

ॐ मन्त्राये नमः

ওঁ মন্ত্রায়ে নমঃ

Oṃ Mantrāye namaḥ

Oṃ we bow to he who is all mantras.

- 49 -

ॐ हविषे नमः

ওঁ হবিষে নমঃ

Oṃ Haviṣe namaḥ

Oṃ we bow to he who is all offerings.

- 50 -

ॐ यज्ञाय नमः

ওঁ য়জ্ঞায় নমঃ

Oṃ Yajñāya namaḥ

Oṃ we bow to he who is all sacrifice.

- 51 -

ॐ पञ्चवक्त्राय नमः

ওঁ পঞ্চবক্ত্রায় নমঃ

Oṃ Pañcavaktrāya namaḥ

Oṃ we bow to he who has five faces.

- 52 -

ॐ सदाशिवाय नमः

ওঁ সদাশিবায় নমঃ

Oṃ Sadāśivāya namaḥ

Oṃ we bow to he who is always the Consciousness of Infinite Goodness.

- 53 -

ॐ विश्वेश्वराय नमः

ওঁ বিশ্বেশ্বরায় নমঃ

Oṃ Viśveśvarāya namaḥ

Oṃ we bow to he who is the supreme lord of the universe.

\- 54 -

ॐ वीरभद्राय नमः

ওঁ বীরভদ্রায় নমঃ

Oṃ Vīrabhadrāya namaḥ

Oṃ we bow to he who is the excellent warrior.

\- 55 -

ॐ गणनाथाय नमः

ওঁ গণনাথায় নমঃ

Oṃ Gaṇanāthāya namaḥ

Oṃ we bow to he who is the lord of the multitudes.

\- 56 -

ॐ प्रजापतये नमः

ওঁ প্রজাপতয়ে নমঃ

Oṃ Prajāpataye namaḥ

Oṃ we bow to he who is the lord of life.

\- 57 -

ॐ हिरण्यरेतसे नमः

ওঁ হিরণ্যরেতসে নমঃ

Oṃ Hiraṇyaretase namaḥ

Oṃ we bow to he who has golden semen.

\- 58 -

ॐ दुर्धर्षाय नमः

ওঁ দুর্ধর্ষায় নমঃ

Oṃ Durdharṣāya namaḥ

Oṃ we bow to he who is difficult to be seen.

\- 59 -

ॐ गिरिशाय नमः

ওঁ গিরিশায় নমঃ

Oṃ Giriśāya namaḥ

Oṃ we bow to he who is of the mountains.

- 60 -

ॐ गिरीशाय नमः

ওঁ গিরীশায় নমঃ

Oṃ Girīśāya namaḥ

Oṃ we bow to he who is lord of the mountains.

- 61 -

ॐ अनघाय नमः

ওঁ অনঘায় নমঃ

Oṃ Anaghāya namaḥ

Oṃ we bow to he who is sinless.

- 62 -

ॐ भुजङ्गभूषणाय नमः

ওঁ ভুজঙ্গভূষণায় নমঃ

Oṃ Bhujaṅga bhūṣaṇāya namaḥ

Oṃ we bow to he who shines like a cobra.

- 63 -

ॐ भर्गाय नमः

ওঁ ভর্গায় নমঃ

Oṃ Bhargāya namaḥ

Oṃ we bow to he who is wealth.

- 64 -

ॐ गिरिधन्विने नमः

ওঁ গিরিধন্বিনে নমঃ

Oṃ Giridhanvine namaḥ

Oṃ we bow to he who is the wealth of the mountains.

- 65 -

ॐ गिरिप्रियाय नमः

ওঁ গিরিপ্রিয়ায় নমঃ

Oṃ Giripriyāya namaḥ

Oṃ we bow to he who is the beloved of the mountains.

- 66 -

ॐ अष्टमूर्त्तये नमः

ওঁ অষ্টমূর্ত্তয়ে নমঃ

Oṃ Aṣṭamūrttaye namaḥ

Oṃ we bow to he who is eight images of divinity.

- 67 -

ॐ अनेकात्मने नमः

ওঁ অনেকাত্মনে নমঃ

Oṃ Anekātmane namaḥ

Oṃ we bow to he who is all souls.

- 68 -

ॐ सात्वकाय नमः

ওঁ সাত্বকায় নমঃ

Oṃ Sātvakāya namaḥ

Oṃ we bow to he who is truth.

- 69 -

ॐ कालाय नमः

ওঁ কালায় নমঃ

Oṃ Kālāya namaḥ

Oṃ we bow to he who is time.

- 70 -

ॐ शाश्वताय नमः

ওঁ শাশ্বতায় নমঃ

Oṃ Śāśvatāya namaḥ

Oṃ we bow to he who is eternal.

- 71 -

ॐ खण्डपरशवे नमः

ওঁ খণ্ডপরশবে নমঃ

Oṃ Khaṇḍaparaśave namaḥ

Oṃ we bow to he who binds divisions in his net.

- 72 -

ॐ अजाय नमः

ওঁ অজায় নমঃ

Oṃ Ajāya namaḥ

Oṃ we bow to he who is unborn.

- 73 -

ॐ रुद्राय नमः

ওঁ রুদ্রায় নমঃ

Oṃ Rudrāya namaḥ

Oṃ we bow to he who relieves suffering.

- 74 -

ॐ कृत्तिवाससे नमः

ওঁ কৃত্তিবাসসে নমঃ

Oṃ Kṛttivāsase namaḥ

Oṃ we bow to he who resides in all action.

- 75 -

ॐ पुराण्टये नमः

ওঁ পুরাণ্টয়ে নমঃ

Oṃ Purāṇṭaye namaḥ

Oṃ we bow to he who is old.

- 76 -

ॐ भगवते नमः

ওঁ ভগবতে নমঃ

Oṃ Bhagavate namaḥ

Oṃ we bow to he who is the supreme divinity.

- 77 -

ॐ प्रमथाधिपाय नमः

ওঁ প্রমথাধিপায় নমঃ

Oṃ Pramathādhipāya namaḥ

Oṃ we bow to he who associates with ghosts and goblins.

- 78 -

ॐ मृत्युञ्जयाय नमः

ওঁ মৃত্যুঞ্জয়ায় নমঃ

Oṃ Mṛtyuñjayāya namaḥ

Oṃ we bow to he who conquers over death.

- 79 -

ॐ शुक्ष्मतनवे नमः

ওঁ শুক্ষ্মতনবে নমঃ

Oṃ Śuksmatanave namaḥ

Oṃ we bow to he who is the subtle body.

- 80 -

ॐ जगद्व्यापिने नमः

ওঁ জগৎব্যাপিনে নমঃ

Oṃ Jagadvyāpine namaḥ

Oṃ we bow to he who distinguishes individuals of the world.

- 81 -

ॐ जगद्गुरवे नमः

ওঁ জগৎগুরবে নমঃ

Oṃ Jagadgurave namaḥ

Oṃ we bow to he who is the guru of the universe.

- 82 -

ॐ सहस्रपदे नमः

ওঁ সহস্রপদে নমঃ

Oṃ Sahasrapade namaḥ

Oṃ we bow to he who has thousands of feet.

- 83 -

ॐ व्योमकेशाय नमः

ওঁ ব্যোমকেশায় নমঃ

Oṃ Vyomakeśāya namaḥ

Oṃ we bow to he whose hair fills the atmosphere.

\- 84 -

ॐ महासेनाय नमः

ওঁ মহাসেনায় নমঃ

Oṃ Mahāsenāya namaḥ

Oṃ we bow to he who is the great general.

\- 85 -

ॐ जनकाय नमः

ওঁ জনকায় নমঃ

Oṃ Janakāya namaḥ

Oṃ we bow to he who is father.

\- 86 -

ॐ चारुविक्रमाय नमः

ওঁ চারুবিক্রমায় নমঃ

Oṃ Cāruvikramāya namaḥ

Oṃ we bow to he whose motion is pleasing.

\- 87 -

ॐ उग्राय नमः

ওঁ উগ্রায় নমঃ

Oṃ Ugrāya namaḥ

Oṃ we bow to he who is terrible.

\- 88 -

ॐ भूपतये नमः

ওঁ ভূপতয়ে নমঃ

Oṃ Bhūpataye namaḥ

Oṃ we bow to he who is the lord of the earth.

\- 89 -

ॐ स्थाणवे नमः

ওঁ স্থাণবে নমঃ

Oṃ Sthāṇave namaḥ

Oṃ we bow to he who is the residence of all.

- 90 -

ॐ ब्रह्मणे नमः

ওঁ ব্রহ্মণে নমঃ

Oṃ Brahmaṇe namaḥ

Oṃ we bow to he who is creative consciousness.

- 91 -

ॐ दिगम्बराय नमः

ওঁ দিগম্বরায় নমঃ

Oṃ Digambarāya namaḥ

Oṃ we bow to he who is clothed in space.

- 92 -

ॐ मृडाय नमः

ওঁ মৃডায় নমঃ

Oṃ Mṛḍāya namaḥ

Oṃ we bow to he who is the object of search.

- 93 -

ॐ पशुपतये नमः

ওঁ পশুপতয়ে নমঃ

Oṃ Paśupataye namaḥ

Oṃ we bow to he who is the lord of animals.

- 94 -

ॐ देवाय नमः

ওঁ দেবায় নমঃ

Oṃ Devāya namaḥ

Oṃ we bow to he who is god.

- 95 -

ॐ महादेवाय नमः

ওঁ মহাদেবায় নমঃ

Oṃ Mahādevāya namaḥ

Oṃ we bow to he who is the great god.

- 96 -

ॐ अव्ययाय नमः

ওঁ অব্যয়ায় নমঃ

Oṃ Avyayāya namaḥ

Oṃ we bow to he who is the imperishable.

- 97 -

ॐ हरये नमः

ওঁ হরয়ে নমঃ

Oṃ Haraye namaḥ

Oṃ we bow to he who takes away all.

- 98 -

ॐ महातेजसे नमः

ওঁ মহাতেজসে নমঃ

Oṃ Mahātejase namaḥ

Oṃ we bow to he who is the great light.

- 99 -

ॐ भगनेत्रभिदे नमः

ওঁ ভগনেত্রভিদে নমঃ

Oṃ Bhaganetrabhide namaḥ

Oṃ we bow to he whose eyes sparkle like a tiger.

- 100 -

ॐ देवदेवाय नमः

ওঁ দেবদেবায় নমঃ

Oṃ Devadevāya namaḥ

Oṃ we bow to he who is the god of gods.

- 101 -

ॐ अव्यग्राय नमः

ওঁ অব্যগ্রায় নমঃ

Oṃ Avyagrāya namaḥ

Oṃ we bow to he who is indifferent.

- 102 -

ॐ अव्यक्ताय नमः

ওঁ অব্যক্তায় নমঃ

Oṃ Avyaktāya namaḥ

Oṃ we bow to he who is indivisible.

- 103 -

ॐ अनन्ताय नमः

ওঁ অনন্তায় নমঃ

Oṃ Anantāya namaḥ

Oṃ we bow to he who is infinite.

- 104 -

ॐ सहस्राक्षाय नमः

ওঁ সহস্রাক্ষায় নমঃ

Oṃ Sahasrākṣāya namaḥ

Oṃ we bow to he who has a thousand eyes.

- 105 -

ॐ मूर्त्तिजाय नमः

ওঁ মূর্ত্তিজায় নমঃ

Oṃ Mūrttijāya namaḥ

Oṃ we bow to he who is the image of victory.

- 106 -

ॐ तारकाय नमः

ওঁ তারকায় নমঃ

Oṃ Tārakāya namaḥ

Oṃ we bow to he who is the illuminator.

- 107 -

ॐ हराय नमः

ওঁ হরায় নমঃ

Oṃ Harāya namaḥ

Oṃ we bow to he within whom all dissolves.

- 108 -

ॐ परमेश्वराय नमः

ওঁ পরমেশ্বরায় নমঃ

Oṃ Parameśvarāya namaḥ

Oṃ we bow to the supreme consciousness.

ॐ नापेश्वराय नमः

ওঁ নাপেশ্বরায় নমঃ

Oṃ Nāpeśvarāya namaḥ

Oṃ we bow to the residence of Dharma.

ॐ नमः ईति

ওঁ নমঃ ঈতি

Oṃ Namaḥ Īti

Oṃ we bow to the completion.

आरति

আরতি

ārati

Dance in Celebration

जय शिव ॐकार । (बोलो) जय शिव ॐकार ।
ब्रह्म विष्णु सदा शिव । अर्धाङ्गि धारा ॥
ॐ हर हर हर महादेव ॥

জয় শিব ওঁকার । (বোলো) জয় শিব ওঁকার ।
ব্রহ্ম বিষ্ণু সদা শিব । অর্দ্ধাঙ্গি ধারা ।।
ওঁ হর হর হর মহাদেব ।।

jaya śiva oṃkāra, (bolo) jaya śiva oṃkāra
brahma viṣṇu sadā śiva, ardhāṅgi dhārā
oṃ hara hara hara mahādeva

Victory to Śiva, the Consciousness of Infinite Goodness, in the form of oṃ. Let's say, Victory to Śiva, the Consciousness of Infinite Goodness, in the form of oṃ. Creative Consciousness, Preserving Consciousness, and always the Consciousness of Continuous Transformation (as well as the Consciousness of Infinite Goodness) who with only His part supports all living beings. oṃ He Who Takes Away, He Who Takes Away, He Who Takes Away, the Great God.

एकानन चरानन पञ्चानन राजे, (शिव) पञ्चानन राजे ।

हंसासन गरुडासन । वृष वाहन ते सोहे ॥

ॐ हर हर हर महादेव ॥

একানন চরানন পঞ্চানন রাজে, (শিব) পঞ্চানন রাজে ।

হংসাসন গরুডাসন । বৃষ বাহন তে সোহে ।।

ওঁ হর হর হর মহাদেব ।।

ekā nana carā nana pañcā nana rāje, (śiva) pañcā nana rāje haṃs
āsana garuḍāsana vṛṣa vāhana te sohe
oṁ hara hara hara mahādeva

He shows Himself with one face, with four faces and with five faces as well, Oh Śiva, with five faces as well. Sitting upon a swan, sitting upon the King of Birds, a golden eagle, sitting upon a bull. oṃ He Who Takes Away, He Who Takes Away, He Who Takes Away, the Great God.

दोय भूज च चतुर्भूज दशभूज ते सोहे, (शिव) दशभूज ते सोहे ।

तीन रूप निराखता । त्रिभुवन जन मोहे ॥

ॐ हर हर हर महादेव ॥

দোয় ভূজ চ চতুর্ভূজ দশভূজ তে সোহে,
(শিব) দশভূজ তে সোহে ।
তীন রূপ নিরাখতা । ত্রিভুবন জন মোহে ।।
ওঁ হর হর হর মহাদেব ।।

doya bhūja ca caturbhūja daśabhūja te sohe,
(śiva) daśabhūja te sohe
tīna rūpa nirākhatā, tri bhuvana jana mohe
oṁ hara hara hara mahādeva

With two arms and with four arms and with ten arms as well, Oh Śiva, with ten arms as well. These three forms revolve, these three forms revolve in the ignorance of the inhabitants of the three worlds. oṃ He Who Takes Away, He Who Takes Away, He Who Takes Away, the Great God.

अक्षर्माला वनमाला रुण्डमाला धारि, (शिव) रुण्डमाला धारि ।
चन्दन मृग मद् चन्द् । भले शुभकारी ॥ ॐ हर हर हर महादेव ॥

অক্ষর্মালা বনমালা রুণ্ডমালা ধারি, (শিব)রুণ্ডমালা ধারি ।
চন্দন মৃগ মদ চন্দ । ভলে শুভকারী ।।
ওঁ হর হর হর মহাদেব ।।

ākṣarmālā vanamālā ruṇḍamālā dhāri, (śiva) ruṇḍamālā dhāri
candana mṛga mada canda, bhale śubha kārī
oṃ hara hara hara mahādeva

With a garland of letters, with a garland of forest flowers, with a garland of skulls as well, Oh Śiva, with a garland of skulls as well. With the scent of sandle, with the scent of musk, with the scent of spiritous liquor as well, truly you are the cause of purification. oṃ He Who Takes Away, He Who Takes Away, He Who Takes Away, the Great God.

श्वेताम्बर पिताम्बर बाघम्बर अङ्गे, (शिव) बाघम्बर अङ्गे ।

सेनतादिक प्रभु तादिक । भूतादिक ते सङ्गे ॥

ॐ हर हर हर महादेव ॥

শ্বেতাম্বর পিতাম্বর বাঘম্বর অঙ্গে,

(শিব) বাঘম্বর অঙ্গে । সেনতাদিক প্রভু তাদিক ।

ভূতাদিক তে সঙ্গে ।। ওঁ হর হর হর মহাদেব ।।

śvetāmbara pitāmbara bāghambara aṅge,
(śiva) bāghambara aṅge
senatādika prabhu tādika, bhūtādika te saṅge
oṃ hara hara hara mahādeva

With a white colored cloth, with a yellow colored cloth, with a tiger skin aparell as well, Oh Śiva, with a tiger skin apparell as well. With an army, as Lord of the armies, with an army, as Lord of the armies, and accompanied by an army of ghosts and goblins as well. oṃ He Who Takes Away, He Who Takes Away, He Who Takes Away, the Great God.

कर मध्ये कमण्डलु चक्र त्रिशूल धरता

(शिव) चक्र त्रिशूल धरता । जगत कर्ता जगत हर्ता ।

जगत पालन कर्ता ॥ ॐ हर हर हर महादेव ॥

কর মধ্যে কমণ্ডলু চক্র ত্রিশূল ধরতা,

(শিব) চক্র ত্রিশূল ধরতা । জগত কর্তা জগত হর্তা ।

জগত পালন কর্তা ।। ওঁ হর হর হর মহাদেব ।।

kara madhye kamaṇḍalu cakra triśūla dharatā,
(śiva) cakra triśūl dharatā, jagat kartā jagat hartā
jagat pālana kartā, oṁ hara hara hara mahādeva

In His hands He holds a water pot, a discus, and a trident as well, Oh Śiva, a discus and a trident as well. He makes the perceivable universe, and He takes away the perceivable universe, and He protects the perceivable universe as well. oṃ He Who Takes Away, He Who Takes Away, He Who Takes Away, the Great God.

ब्रह्म विष्णु सदाशिव जनत आविवेका, (शिव) जनत आविवेका ।

प्रनव आक्षर ॐमध्ये । ये तीनो एका ॥ ॐ हर हर हर महादेव ॥

ব্রহ্ম বিষ্ণু সদা শিব জনত আবিবেকা,

(শিব) জনত আবিবেকা । প্রনব আক্ষর ওঁ মধ্যে ।

য়ে তীনো একা ।। ওঁ হর হর হর মহাদেব ।।

brahma viṣṇu sadāśiva janata āvivekā, (śiva) janata āvivekā
pranav ākṣar oṁ madhye, ye tīna ekā
oṃ hara hara hara mahādeva

Creative Conciousness, Preserving Consciousness, and always the Consciousness of Continuous Transformation (as well as the Consciousness of Infinite Goodness), to those people without discrimination (appear separate). But within the holy syllable oṃ, but within the holy syllable oṃ, the three are actually ONE. oṃ He Who Takes Away, He Who Takes Away, He Who Takes Away, the Great God.

त्रिगुण स्वामि कि आरति यो कोइ नर गावे,

(शिव) यो कोइ नर गावे । बनात शिवानन्द स्वामि ।

वञ्चित फल पह्वे ॥ ॐ हर हर हर महादेव ॥

ত্রিগুণ স্বামি কি আরতি য়ো কোই নর গাবে ।

(শিব) য়ো কোই নর গাবে । বনাত শিবানন্দ স্বামি । বাঞ্চিত

ফল পহ্বে ।। ওঁ হর হর হর মহাদেব ।।

triguṇa svāmi ki ārati yo koi nara gāve,
(śiva) yo koi nara gāve, banāta śivānanda svāmi
vañcita phala pahve, oṁ hara hara hara mahādeva

Whatever man will sing this praise of the Master of the three gunas (qualities), Oh Śiva, whatever man will sing. Make him a master of the Bliss of Infinite Consciousness, make him a master of the Bliss of Infinite Consciousness, certainly that will be the fruit he receives. oṃ He Who Takes Away, He Who Takes Away, He Who Takes Away, the Great God.

जय शिव ॐकार । (बोलो) जय शिव ॐकार । ब्रह्म विष्णु सदा शिव । अर्धाङ्गि धारा ॥ ॐ हर हर हर महादेव ॥

জয় শিব ওঁকার । (বোলো) জয় শিব ওঁকার । ব্রহ্ম বিষ্ণু সদা শিব । অর্দ্ধাঙ্গি ধারা ।। ওঁ হর হর হর মহাদেব ।।

jaya śiva oṃkāra, (bolo) jaya śiva oṃkāra
brahma viṣṇu sadā śiva, ardhāṅgi dhārā
oṃ hara hara hara mahādeva

Victory to Śiva, the Consciousness of Infinite Goodness, in the form of oṃ. Let's say, Victory to Śiva, the Consciousness of Infinite Goodness, in the form of oṃ. Creative Consciousness, Preserving Consciousness, and always the Consciousness of Continuous Transformation (as well as the Consciousness of Infinite Goodness) who with only His part supports all living beings. oṃ He Who Takes Away, He Who Takes Away, He Who Takes Away, the Great God.

ॐ महादेव महात्रान महायोगि महेश्वर ।
सर्वपाप हरां देव मकाराय नमो नमः ॥

ওঁ মহাদেব মহাত্রান মহায়োগি মহেশ্বর ।
সর্বপাপ হরাং দেব মকারায় নমো নমঃ ।।

oṃ mahādeva mahātrāna mahāyogi maheśvara
sarvapāpa harāṃ deva makārāya namo namaḥ

oṃ The Great God, the Great Reliever, the Great Yogi, Oh Supreme Lord, Oh God who removes all Sin, in the form of the letter **M** which dissolves creation, we bow to you again and again.

ॐ नमः शिवाय शान्ताय कारणत्राय हेतवे ।

निवेदायामि चत्मनं त्वं गति परमेश्वर ॥

ওঁ নমঃ শিবায় শান্তায় কারণত্রায় হেতবে ।

নিবেদায়ামি চত্মনং ত্বং গতি পরমেশ্বর ।।

oṃ namaḥ śivāya śāntāya kāraṇatrāya hetave
nivedāyāmi catmanaṃ tvaṃ gati parameśvara

oṃ I bow to the Consciousness of Infinite Goodness, to Peace, to the Cause of the three worlds, I offer to you the fullness of my soul, Oh Supreme Lord.

ॐ नमः शिवाय ।

ওঁ নমঃ শিবায় ।

oṃ namaḥ śivāya ||

oṃ I bow to the Consciousness of Infinite Goodness

अथ शिव चालीसा

दोहा

जय गणेश गिरिजा सुवन मङ्गल मूल सुजान ।
कहत अयोद्यादास तुम देहु अभय वरदान ॥
उमापति महादेव कि जय

चौपाई

जय गिरिजापति दीन दयाला । सदा करत सन्तन प्रतिपाला ॥
भाला चन्द्रमा सोहत नीके । कानन कुण्डल नागफनी के ॥
अङ्ग गौर शिर गङ्ग बहाये । मुण्डमाल तन छार लगाये ॥
वस्त्र खाल बाघम्बर सोहे । छवि को देख नाग मुनि मोहे ॥
मैना मातु को हवे दुलारी । बाम अङ्ग सोहत छवि न्यारी ॥
कर त्रिशूल बाघम्बर धारी । करत सदा शत्रुन क्षयकारी ॥
नन्दि गणेश सोहैं तहँ कैसे । सागर मद्ये कमल हैं जैसे ॥
कार्तिक श्याम और गणराऊ । या छवि को कहि जात न काऊ ॥
देवन जबहीं जाय पुकारा । तबही दुःख प्रभु आप निवारा ॥
किया उपद्रव तारक भारी । देवन सब मिलि तुमहिं जुहारी ॥
तुरत षडानन आप पठायउ । लव निमेष महँ मारि गिरायउ ॥
आप जलंधर असुर संहारा । सुयश तुम्हार विदित संसारा ॥
त्रिपुरासुर सन युद्ध मचायी । सबहिं कृपा कर लीन बचायी ॥
किया तपहिं भागीरथ भारी । पुरब प्रतिज्ञा तासु पुरारी ॥
दानिन महँ तुम सम कोउ नाहिं । सेवक स्तुति करत सदाहीं ॥
वेद नाम महिमा तव गाई । अकथ अनादि भेद नहिं पाई ॥
प्रकट उदधि मन्थन में ज्वाला । जरत सुरासुर भये विहाला ॥

कीन्ह दया तहँ करी सहाई । नीलाकंहु तब नाम कहाई ॥

पूजन रामचन्द्र जब कीन्हां । जीत के लंक विभीषण दीन्हा ॥

सहस कमल में हो रहे धारी । कीन्ह परीक्षा तबहिं पुरारी ॥

एक कमल प्रभु राखेउ जोई । कमल नयन पूजन चहं सोई ॥

कठिन भक्ति देखी प्रभु शंकर । भये प्रसन्न दिये ईच्छित वर ॥

जय जय जय अनंत अविनाशी । करत कृपा सब के घटवासी ॥

दुष्ट सकल नित मोहि सतावै । भ्रमत रहे मोहि चैन न आवे ॥

त्राहि त्राहि मैं नाथ पुकारो । यहि अवसर मोहि आन उबारो ॥

लै त्रिशूल शत्रुन को मारो । संकट से मोहि आन उबारो ॥

मातु पिता भ्राता सब कोई । संकट में पूछत नहिं कोई ॥

स्वामी एक है आस तुम्हारी । आय हरहु अब संकट भारी ॥

धन निरधन को देत सदाहीं । जो कोई जांचे सो फल पाहीं ॥

अस्तुति केहि विधि करौं तुम्हारी । क्षमहु नाथ अब चूक हमारी ॥

शंकर हो संकट के नाशन । मङ्गल कारण विघ्न विनाशन ॥

योगी यति मुनि द्यान लगावैं । नारद शारद शीश नवावैं ॥

नमो नमो जय नमो शिवाय । सुर ब्रह्मादिक पार न पाय ॥

जो यह पाठ करे मन लाई । ता पार होत है शम्भु सहाई ॥

ऋनिया जो कोई हो अधिकारी । पाठ करे सो पावनहारी ॥

पुत्र हीन करे ईच्छा कोई । निश्चय शिव प्रसाद तेहि होई ॥

पण्डित त्रयोदशी को लावे । द्यान पूर्वक होम करावे ॥

त्रयोदशी व्रत करे हमेशा । तन नहीं ताके रहे क्लेशा ॥

धूप दीप नैवेद्य चढावे । संकर सन्मुख पाठ सुनावे ॥

जन्म जन्म के पाप नसावे । अन्तवास शिवपुर में पावे ॥

कहै अयोद्या आस तुम्हारी । जानि सकल दुःख हरहु हमारी ॥

दोहा

नित्त नेम कर प्रातः ही पाठ करौ चालीस ।

तुम मेरी मनोकामना पूर्ण करो जगदीश ॥

उमापति महादेव कि जय

হিব পূজা Śiva Pūjā শিব পূজা

অথ শিব চালীসা

দোহা

জয় গণেশ গিরিজা সুবন মঙ্গল মূল সুজান ।
কহত অয়োদ্যাদাস তুম দেহু অভয় বরদান ।।
উমাপতি মহাদেব কি জয়

চৌপাঈ

জয় গিরিজাপতি দীন দয়ালা । সদা করত সন্তন প্রতিপালা ।।
ভালা চন্দ্রমা সোহত নীকে । কানন কুণ্ডল নাগফনী কে ।।
অঙ্গগৌর শির গঙ্গ বহায়ে । মুণ্ডমাল তন ছার লগায়ে ।।
বস্ত্র খাল বাঘম্বর সোহে । ছবি কো দেখ নাগ মুনি মোহে ।।
মৈনা মাতু কো হবে দুলারী । বাম অঙ্গ সোহত ছবি ন্যারী ।।
কর ত্রিশূল বাঘম্বর ধারী । করত সদা শত্রুন ক্ষয়কারী ।।
নন্দি গণেশ সোহৈং তহঁ কৈসে । সাগর মদ্যে কমল হৈং জৈসে ।।
কার্তিক শ্যাম ঔর গণরাউ । য়া ছবি কো কহি জাত ন কাউ।।
দেবন জবহীং জায় পুকারা । তবহী দুঃখ প্রভু আপ নিবারা ।।
কিয়া উপদ্রব তারক ভারী । দেবন সব মিলি তুমহিং জুহারী ।।
তুরত ষডানন আপ পঠায়উ । লব নিমেষ মহঁ মারি গিরায়উ ।।
আপ জলংধর অসুর সংহারা । সুয়শ তুম্হার বিদিত সংসারা ।।
ত্রিপুরাসুর সন যুদ্ধ মচায়ী । সবহিং কৃপা কর লীন বচায়ী ।।
কিয়া তপহিং ভাগীরথ ভারী । পুরব প্রতিজ্ঞা তাসু পুরারী ।।
দানিন মহঁ তুম সম কোউ নাহিং । সেবক স্তুতি করত সদাহীং ।।
বেদ নাম মহিমা তব গাঈ । অকথ অনাদি ভেদ নহিং পাঈ ।।
প্রকট উদধি মন্থন মেং জ্বালা । জরত সুরাসুর ভয়ে বিহালা ।।
কীন্হ দয়া তহঁ করী সহাঈ । নীলাকংহু তব নাম কহাঈ ।।
পূজন রামচন্দ্র জব কীন্হাং । জীত কে লংক বিভীষণ দীন্হা ।।
সহস কমল মেং হো রহে ধারী । কীন্হ পরীক্ষা তবহিং পুরারী ।।
এক কমল প্রভু রাখেউ জাঈ । কমল নয়ন পূজন চহং সোঈ ।।

কঠিন ভক্তি দেখী প্রভু শংকর । ভয়ে প্রসন্ন দিয়ে ঈচ্ছিত বর ।।
জয় জয় জয় অনংত অবিনাশী । করত কৃপা সব কে ঘটবাসী ।।
দুষ্ট সকল নিত মোহি সতাবৈ । ভ্রমত রহে মোহি চৈন ন আবে ।।
ত্রাহি ত্রাহি মৈং নাথ পুকারা । য়হি অবসর মোহি আন উবারা ।।
লৈ ত্রিশূল শত্রুন কো মারো । সংকট সে মোহি আন উবারো ।।
মাতু পিতা ভ্রাতা সব কোঈ । সংকট মেং পূছত নহিং কোঈ ।।
স্বামী এক হৈ আস তুম্হারী । আয় হরহু অব সংকট ভারী ।।
ধন নিরধন কো দেত সদাহীং । জো কোঈ জাংচে সো ফল পাহীং ।।
অস্তুতি কেহি বিধি করৌং তুম্হারী । ক্ষমহু নাথ অব চূক হমারী ।।
শংকর হো সংকট কে নাশন । মঙ্গল কারণ বিঘ্ন বিনাশন ।।
য়োগী য়তি মুনি দ্যান লগাবৈং । নারদ শারদ শীশ নবাবৈং ।।
নমো নমো জয় নমো শিবায় । সুর ব্রহ্মাদিক পার ন পায় ।।
জো য়হ পাঠ করে মন লাঈ । তা পার হোত হৈ শম্ভু সহাঈ ।।
ঋনিয়া জো কোঈ হো অধিকারী । পাঠ করে সা পাবনহারী ।।
পুত্র হীন করে ঈচ্ছা কোঈ । নিশ্চয় শিব প্রসাদ তেহি হোঈ ।।
পণ্ডিত ত্রয়োদশী কো লাবে । দ্যান পূর্বক হোম করাবে ।।
ত্রয়োদশী ব্রত করে হমেশা । তন নহীং তাকে রহে কলেশা ।।
ধূপ দীপ নৈবেদ্য চঢাবে । সংকর সন্মুখ পাঠ সুনাবে ।।
জন্ম জন্ম কে পাপ নসাবে । অন্তবাস শিবপুর মেং পাবে ।।
কহৈ অয়োদ্যা আস তুম্হারী । জানি সকল দুঃখ হরহু হমারী ।।

দোহা

নিত্ত নেম কর প্রাতঃ হী পাঠ করৌ চালীস ।
তুম মেরী মনোকামনা পূর্ণ করো জগদীশ ।।
উমাপতি মহাদেব কি জয়

atha śiva cālīsā

loha

aya gaṇeśa girijā suvana maṅgala mūla sujāna
kahata ayodyādāsa tum dehu abhaya varadāna
umāpati mahādeva ki jaya

caupāī

jaya girijāpati dīna dayālā
sadā karata santana pratipālā
bhālā candramā sohata nīke
kānana kuṅḍala nāgaphanī ke
aṅga gaura śira gaṅga bahāye
muṇḍamāla tana chāra lagāye
vastra khāla bāghambara sohe
chavi ko dekha nāga muni mohe
mainā mātu ko have dulārī
bāma aṅga sohata chavi nyārī
kara triśūla bāghambara dhārī
karata sadā śatruna kṣaya kārī
nandi gaṇeśa sohaiṃ tahaṁ kaise
sāgara madye kamala haiṃ jaise
kārtika śyāma aur gaṇarāū
yā chavi ko kahi jāta na kāū
devana jabahīṃ jāya pukārā
tabahī duḥkha prabhu āpa nivārā
kiyā upadrava tāraka bhārī
devana saba mili tumahiṃ juhārī
turata ṣaḍānana āpa paṭhāyau
lava nimeṣa mahaṁ māri girāyau
āpa jalaṃdhar asura saṃhārā
suyaśa tumhāra vidita saṃsārā

tripurāsura sana yuddha macāyī
sabahiṃ kṛpā kara līna bacāyī
kiyā tapahiṃ bhāgīratha bhārī
puraba pratijñā tāsu purārī
dānina mahaṁ tuma sama kou nāhiṃ
sevaka stuti karata sadāhīṃ
veda nāma mahimā tava gāī
akatha anādi bheda nahiṃ pāī
prakaṭa udadhi mathana meṃ jvālā
jarata surāsura bhaye vihālā
kīnha dayā tahaṁ karī sahāī
nīlākaṃhu taba nāma kahāī
pūjana rāmacandra jaba kīnhāṃ
jīta ke laṃka vibhīṣaṇa dīnhā
sahasa kamala meṃ ho rahe dhārī
kīnha parīkṣā tabahiṃ purārī
eka kamala prabhu rākheu joī
kamala nayana pūjana cahaṃ soī
kaṭhina bhakti dekhī prabhu śaṃkara
bhaye prasanna diye īcchita vara
jaya jaya jaya anaṃta avināśī
karata kṛpā saba ke ghaṭavāsī
duṣṭa sakala nita mohi satāvai
bhramata rahe mohi caina na āve
trāhi trāhi maiṃ nātha pukāro
yahi avasara mohi āna ubāro
lai triśūla śatruna ko māro
saṃkaṭa se mohi āna ubāro
mātu pitā bhrātā saba koī
saṃkaṭa meṃ pūchata nahiṃ koī

svāmī eka hai āsa tumhārī
āya harahu aba saṃkaṭa bhārī
dhana niradhana ko deta sadāhīṃ
jo koī jāṃce so phala pāhīṃ
astuti kehi vidhi karauṃ tumhārī
kṣamahu nātha aba cūka hamārī
śaṃkara ho saṃkaṭa ke nāśan
maṅgala kāraṇa vighna vināśana
yogī yati muni dyāna lagāvaiṃ
nārada śārada śīśa navāvaiṃ
namo namo jaya namo śivāya
sura brahmādika pāra na pāya
jo yaha pāṭha kare mana lāī
tā pāra hota hai śambhu sahāī
ṛniyā jo koī ho adhikārī
pāṭha kare so pāvanahārī
putra hīna kare īcchā koī
niścaya śiva prasāda tehi hoī
paṇḍita trayodaśī ko lāve
dyāna pūrvaka homa karāve
trayodaśī vrata kare hameśā
tana nahīṃ tāke rahe kaleśā
dhūpa dīpa naivedya caḍhāve
saṃkara sanmukha pāṭha sunāve
janma janma ke pāpa nasāve
antavāsa śivapura meṃ pāve
kahai ayodyā āsa tumhārī
jāni sakala duḥkha harahu hamārī

dohā
nitta nema kara prāṭha hī pāṭha karau cālīsa
tuma merī manokāmanā pūrṇa karo jagadīśa
umāpati mahādeva ki jaya

atha śiva cālīsā

Dohā:
Praise to Ganesha, the son of She who is born of the mountain, the excellent one, who is the root of all welfare. It is said that you are the servant of Peace (Ayodyā, the devotee who sings the song). Give to us the blessing of freedom from fear.

Chaupai:
Praise to the Lord of She who is born of the mountain (Śiva), who is kind and compassionate to the poor, who always protects his children.
Upon whose forehead the moon is shining elegantly, and whose ears are ornamented by rings of cobra snakes.
His body is white, and upon his head the Ganga river is flowing.
He wears a garland of skulls, and covers his body with ashes.
He wears a tiger skin garment, and his countenance appears fascinating as a naked ascetic.
To the mother maina bird, he is as a beloved daughter. His left side shines with a female countenance.
In his hand the tiger skin clad One (Shiva) holds a trident. Always he destroys all that is enemical.
How are Nandi and Ganesh always there before you? Just like the lotus is in the midst of the water.
Kartik and the dark one and others of the multitude (of divine beings), (will not be able to see) this countenance manifested in another form or any other place.
Whenever the Gods make a shout for victory, then, Oh Lord, you prevent all pain.

When that great disturbance was caused by the Asura Tāraka, all the Gods united in worship to you.
Quickly you dispatched the six faced one (Kartikeya), and between the moments of a twinkling of an eye, he was thrown down to his death.
You defeated the demon Jalandhara, making your excellent welfare know to the Sansara, the world of objects and relationships.
You made war against Tripurasura, and saved everyone by the grace of your absorption.
Oh Purari, resident of the City (a name of Śiva), what a great spiritual discipline Bhagiratha performed to complete his promise.
There is no other comparable to your generous nature, and your devotees always sing your praises.
The Vedas sing the greatness of your name, but the eternal, ever-existant, indescribable is not found in the manifestations of division.
Your light manifested in the churning of the ocean, removing the ancient fear of both Gods and asuras.
With what compassion you offered assistance there, when they called the name of the Blue-necked One.
When Ramachandra performed worship, you gave him Vibhiṣaṇa to defeat Laṅka.
Oh Purari, you performed the test of holding a thousand lotuses.
Oh Lord, who placed that one lotus there? It was the same lotus-eyed one who desired the puja.
Oh Lord Śaṅkara, the Cause of Peace, seeing his difficult austerities of devotion, being pleased you gave him the desired boon.
Victory, Victory, Victory to the Infinite who is Indestructible.
Give your grace to all the residents of creation.
Every day my evil-mind is troubled. I continue in confusion and ignorance, and consciousness does not come to me.
Save me, save me, Oh Lord! Hear my call! Raise me up at this time.
Kill the enemies with your trident, and raise me up above all pain.

Mother, father, brothers, nor any others, do not even ask me about my pain.
You are the only refuge, oh Master. Now take away the great weight of my pain.
You give to the rich and you give to the poor. Whoever comes in want, to him it is given.
I have no such capacity to sing your praises. Whatever mistakes I have made, please forgive them all.
Śaṅkara, Oh Cause of Peace, you are the destroyer of all pain, the cause of welfare, and destroyer of obstacles.
Yogis, ascetics, and great wise beings, meditate upon you, as well as Narad and Śarad bow their heads to you.
I bow, I bow, Victory! I bow to Śiva! The Gods and Brahma and other divine beings cannot discover the end of your infinity.
Whoever will recite this song with one point of mind, Śambhu, the giver of bliss, will always protect.
Debtors or others who are in want of Śiva's blessings, if they recite this song, will certainly receive according to their desires.
Whoever is without children and desirous of a child, without a doubt, Śiva will grant fulfillment to them.
The wise and learned ones perform the vow of worship on the thirteenth day, and meditate and perform the fire sacrifice for Lord Śiva.
Who always performs the vow of worship on the thirteenth day, his body will continue to be free from pain.
Offerings of incense, lights and food will be made, and this recitation will be made in front of Lord Śiva.
Sins of many births will be destroyed, and at last you will reside in the city of Śiva.
This is the expectation of your devotee (Ayodya name); I know you will remove all pain from me.

Doha:
If one will always recite this song of praise in the early morning of every day, every desire will be fulfilled, Oh Lord of the Universe.

More Books by Shree Maa and Swami Satyananda Saraswati

Annapūrṇa Thousand Names
Before Becoming This
Bhagavad Gītā
Chaṇḍi Pāṭh
Cosmic Pūjā
Cosmic Pūjā Bengali
Devī Gītā
Devī Mandir Songbook
Durgā Pūjā Beginner
Ganeśa Pūjā
Gems From the Chaṇḍi
Guru Gītā
Hanumān Pūjā
Kālī Dhyānam
Kālī Pūjā
Lakṣmī Sahasra Nāma
Lalitā Triśati
Rudrāṣṭādhyāyī
Sahib Sadhu
Saraswati Pūjā for Children
Shree Maa's Favorite Recipes
Shree Maa - The Guru & the Goddess
Shree Maa, The Life of a Saint
Śiva Pūjā Beginner
Śiva Pūjā and Advanced Fire Ceremony
Sundara Kāṇḍa
Swāmī Purāṇa
Thousand Names of Ganeśa
Thousand Names of Gayatri
Thousand Names of Viṣṇu and
Satya Nārāyaṇa Vrata Kathā

CDs and Cassettes

Chaṇḍi Pāṭh
Durgā Pūjā Beginner
Lalitā Triśati
Mantras of the Nine Planets
Navarṇa Mantra
Oh Dark Night Mother
Oṃ Mantra
Sādhu Stories from the Himalayas
Shree Maa at the Devi Mandir
Shree Maa in the Temple of the Heart
Shiva is in My Heart
Shree Maa on Tour, 1998
Śiva Pūjā Beginner
Śiva Pūjā and Advanced Fire Ceremony
The Goddess is Everywhere
The Songs of Ramprasad
The Thousand Names of Kālī
Tryambakaṃ Mantra

Videos

Across the States with Shree Maa & Swamiji
Meaning and Method of Worship
Shree Maa: Meeting a Modern Saint
Visiting India with Shree Maa and Swamiji

Please visit us at www.shreemaa.org
Our email is info@shreemaa.org

Lightning Source UK Ltd.
Milton Keynes UK
UKHW010844280721
387905UK00001B/120

9 781887 472883